HEALTHKINS HELP

by Jane Belk Moncure
illustrated by Lois Axeman

ELGIN, ILLINOIS 60120

Distributed by Childrens Press, 1224 West Van Buren Street, Chicago, Illinois 60607.

Library of Congress Cataloging in Publication Data

Moncure, Jane Belk.
  Healthkins help.

  Summary: The Healthkin king and queen advise on cleanliness, proper dental care, exercise, and other healthful habits.
  1. Health—Juvenile literature. [1. Health]
I. Axeman, Lois, ill. II. Title.
RA777.M657   1982   613′.0432   82-14713
ISBN 0-89565-242-0

© 1982 The Child's World, Inc.
All rights reserved. Printed in U.S.A.

1 2 3 4 5 6 7 8 9 10 11 12 R 89 88 87 86 85 84 83 82

HEALTHKINS HELP

Meet the Healthkins' King and Queen.

Their Healthkin magic will keep you clean!

Bubbly-scrubbly-
zippety-zoap!

The Queen makes magic
with a bar of soap.

Jump into a shower; slide into a tub.
Soap makes magic as you scrub.

Dirt disappears
   from hands and ears . . .

   from head to toes . . .
      from both elbows!

When you are presented to the King, he'll say,

"Zippety-zoe-zippety-zean!

I hereby dub you—'Healthkin-clean!' "

Bristly-brushly-zippety-zush!
The Queen makes magic
with a fluffy toothbrush.

Brush as she says—
the way your teeth grow.

"Brush up
like a rocket,

"down like
the rain,

"We Healthkins know how to brush.

"brush back and forth—
like the Healthkin Food Train!"

"Brush your teeth three times a day
to keep those cavities away.
Keep your teeth sunshine clean—
from top to bottom and in between!"

"And by the way,"
says the Healthkin King,

"instead of sticky,
gooey sweets—

chew apples and celery for snacks and treats."

"Now hear this!" say the King and Queen.
"We make all kinds of great surprises
to help our friends do exercises!"

"We make things for pushing,

pulling,

throwing

pumping,

climbing,

sliding,

jogging,

jumping.

"Zippety-zappety-zumpety-zong!
　　Exercise will keep you strong.

　　Exercise your muscles every day.
　　Stretch and bend
　　　　　　　the Healthkin way!"

"And there's still more," says the Healthkin Queen.

"Join the Healthkins! They need fresh air—

and plenty of rest—

so they can be their Healthkin best!"

"And every day in sun or rain,
they eat good food—

from the Healthkin Food Train."

Once a year in the middle of May,
the Healthkins have a special day.
They invite all kinds of health helpers—

doctors, dentists,

28

nurses, too,
pharmacists,
therapists, to name a few.

But do you know who
your best health helper is?

Can you guess?
You—yes, you!

Take care of yourself. Do your best.
Other health helpers will do the rest.